Know-It-All Library

Prehistoric Animals

By Edward J. Zagorski

The Know-It-All Library
ROURKE ENTERPRISES, INC.
Windermere, Florida 32786

Contents

COVER The Iguanadon and Stegosaurus are dinosaurs that lived in different times, or eras. Stegosaurus (also on page 7) was one of the early dinosaurs. Iguanadon, standing upright, was one of the later dinosaurs that lived about 70 million years ago.

Published by Rourke Enterprises, Inc., PO Box 929, Windermere, FL 32786. Printed in the United States of America.

Library of Congress Cataloging in Publication Data

Zagorski, Edward J.
Prehistoric animals.

(Know-it-all library)
Summary: Describes twenty kinds of dinosaur and other ancient animals that inhabited the earth from 250 million to 50,000 years ago.
1. Palenthology—Juvenile literature [1. Extinct animals. 2. Dinosaurs]
I. Title II. Series
QE714.5.Z34 566 82-22738
ISBN 0-86592-708-1 AACR2

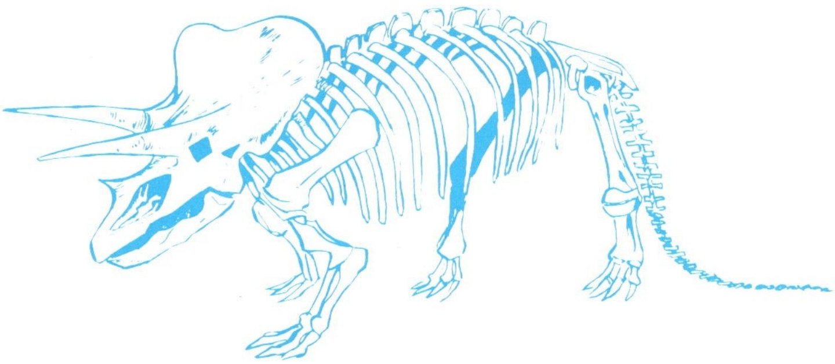

A Long Time Ago . . .

. . . no human being walked the earth. Only insects flew the skies. All other animals either swam in the oceans or crawled on the land.

We know about these creatures today because of their *fossils.* Fossils are traces of ancient animals bones, teeth, and footprints. They have been found in almost every part of the world. Because of these fossil clues, scientists have a very good idea of what these animals looked like and how they lived.

The most famous of all prehistoric animals are, of course, the dinosaurs. They came in many shapes and sizes. Some were immense — the largest animals ever — and some were tiny. Some had armor-like skin, some had horns, and others had scales.

All dinosaurs were reptiles — the same as today's lizards, crocodiles, snakes, and turtles. Dinosaurs laid eggs, had air-breathing lungs, and most were cold-blooded.

Scientists believe that dinosaurs roamed and ruled the earth for about 160 million years. We're not sure why they died out, but it is known that dinosaurs became extinct about 65 million years ago.

Then mammals took over the world. Mammals are warm-blooded, and, unlike the dinosaurs, mammals could live in very cold weather.

In the following pages, you will be able to see what some of the most interesting prehistoric animals looked like and what their world looked like.

Edaphosaurus

■ Lived about 230 million years ago ■

The Edaphosaurus was a reptile that lived before any dinosaurs had appeared on earth. It sometimes grew to a length of 12 feet. Edaphosaurus moved about on short legs. It had a huge, skin-covered fin on its back that was held up by bony spines. Its head was small, and its teeth were blunt — not pointy or sharp. Its feet had sharp claws. Though it was scary-looking, it really was a gentle animal. It ate only plants.

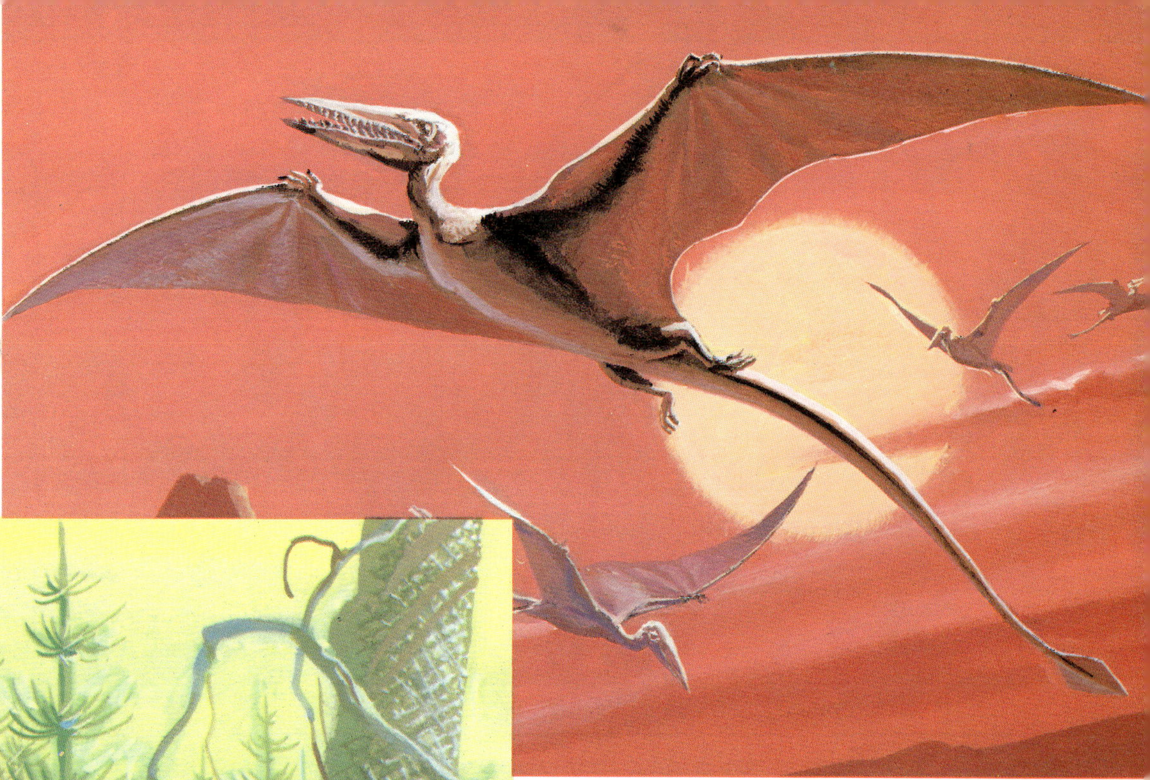

Rhamphorhynchus

■ Lived about 180 million years ago ■

The Rhamphorhynchus was a flying reptile that had a wing-spread of about 4 feet. The leaf-shaped piece of skin at the end of its long, thin tail acted as a kind of rudder when it flew. Rhamphorhynchus had a low skull with long rows of fairly large teeth. And it had claws at the front of each wing. This allowed it to grasp the branches of trees. Scientists believe that this animal hung upside down from branches, much as bats do today.

Mastodonsaurus

■ Lived about 160 million years ago ■

The Mastodonsaurus was the largest of all amphibians to live on earth. It could live part of the time in water and part of the time on land. Some grew to 15 feet in length. This animal's head, shaped like a triangle, could be as long as 3 feet. Its body was covered by hard and bony growths that ran in lines along the back, but scattered on the sides. Its legs and tail were small for its large body.

Stegosaurus

■ Lived about 150 million years ago ■

The Stegosaurus was a frightening animal. It grew to 25 feet long, about 13 feet high, and it weighed 7 to 10 tons. Its head was flat and low, and its jaws held close to 100 small teeth. Stegosaurus lived among trees and fed on soft plants. Its body was huge and had tough, armor plates sticking up along its back. Because of its bulky weight, it could not move very fast. But its main weapon against attackers was its strong tail that had two-foot long spikes.

Brontosaurus

■ Lived about 135 million years ago ■

The Brontosaurus lived in swamps and streams. It was huge — about 75 feet long and weighed close to 40 tons. It had a long flexible neck and a massive tail that ended in a whiplash tip. It could move about in water without trouble and could come to the surface easily, even from depths of 42 feet. Its legs formed thick columns, and its feet were as much as 26 inches wide. The toes had long claws. Brontosaurus did not eat meat. It liked to nibble on plants.

Trachodon

■ Lived about 130 million years ago ■

The Trachodon was a duck-billed dinosaur that stood about 18 feet high and was about 30 feet long. It walked in a stooping position and often dropped to all four feet. Its feet were webbed. Trachodon probably spent most of its time in the water, eating plants. Its thin skin was wrinkled and covered with scales. The name Trachodon means *rough tooth*. It is believed that this animal had more than 1,000 teeth in its long and flat mouth.

Pteranodon

■ Lived about 130 million years ago ■

The Pteranodon was a short-tailed flying reptile. Its head sometimes reached up to 75 inches in length. And its huge beak was sometimes 3 feet long. Its neck was also long and very strong. Its wings could spread as wide as 27 feet and were supported by strong limbs. The Pteranodon fed mostly on fish. Its lower jaw had a large pouch to store food until it could be swallowed and digested.

Tyrannosaurus

■ Lived about 100 million years ago ■

The Tyrannosaurus was a savage, meat-eating animal that stood on its massive and powerful hind legs. Its name come from the Greek and means *tyrant-lizard*. It measured 19 feet tall and 47 feet long — from the tip of its nose to the end of its mighty tail. Its knee was 6 feet above ground, and the claws on its hind feet were as long as 6 to 8 inches. Its teeth were well-developed — sharp as blades and 3 to 6 inches long and an inch wide!

Styracosaurus

■ Lived about 80 million years ago ■

The Styracosaurus walked on all four legs, unlike most other reptile dinosaurs. It and the Triceratops (on the next page) belonged to the same family. The Styracosaurus was about 20 feet long. It had six horn-covered spikes jutting out from a bony shield covering its neck. There was another horn above it nose. Its whole back was covered with bumps. Styracosaurus kept enemies away by using its drooping tail as a weapon.

Tylosaurus

■ Lived about 80 million years ago ■

The Tylosaurus was a lively swimmer. It had a long body that could reach 30 feet in length. Its tail was flat and its feet were wide, webbed paddles. It had two rows of stong teeth, very much like some crocodiles. Tylosaurus had a big head and a sharp, pointed snout. A crest grew from the top of its head to its tail. This animal used its tail to stun its prey. It then usually swallowed its food in one whole piece.

Triceratops

■ Lived about 80 million years ago ■

The Triceratops was a short, heavy dinosaur. It was sometimes 26 feet long, but only 8 to 10 feet high, and could weigh as much as 12 tons. Its head had two powerful horns above the eyes and another horn just above the nose. Its neck was protected by a shield of hard skin. With its dangerous, powerful horns and sturdy legs, Triceratops could rush under attacking meat-eaters and defend itself with its horns. It was sometimes attacked by Tyrannosaurus.

Elasmosaurus

■ Lived about 65 million years ago ■

The Elasmosaurus was a colossal sea reptile that lived in the waters that covered central Europe and America. It was at home in the sea because it was

easier for it to move its huge body in water rather than on land. Some of these animals measured up to 50 feet in length. Their feet were flat and used as paddles. Elasmosaurus fed by catching large numbers of fish and chewing them with its long rows of sharp, pointy teeth.

Brontotherium

■ Lived about 36 million years ago ■

The Brontotherium also belonged to the rhinoceros family. It was more than 7 feet tall and sometimes up to 16 feet long. It had a massive, broad body and thick legs. It could weigh up to 5 tons. Brontotherium had a remarkable forked horn on its nose at the end of its snout. This animal was probably not a meat-eater since it had poor teeth. Instead, it pulled leaves from tall shrubs and low trees with its lips. It then used its grinding teeth in back to chew.

Dwarf Rhinoceros

■ Lived about 30 million years ago ■

The Dwarf Rhinoceros had brains that were one-tenth the size of those of today's rhinos. It had a thick, heavy body and weighed about 3 or 4 tons. Its massive legs had stubby feet that bore hoof-like toes. This animal had two bony horns that grew side by side above the nose. These were powerful weapons when coupled with the animal's weight behind them. Whole herds of these small rhinos died in sand drifts or marshes.

Machairodus

■ Lived about 30 million years ago ■

The Machairodus was a prehistoric, saber-toothed member of the cat family. Its name comes from the Greek and means *knife-and-tooth*. Its top two canine teeth were long and as sharp as knives. These were powerful weapons that could be used as daggers. This animal also had sharp claws on its feet. Machairodus, a fierce hunter, lived in Asia and Europe.

Phororhacos

■ Lived about 25 million years ago ■

The Phororhacos was a meat-eating bird that lived in South America. It had small wings and could not fly, but it was a very good runner. It was able to run after its prey for hours. This bird could reach heights of about 6 feet and had a powerful hooked beak. This gave it a savage and frightening look. It had long legs, each ending in a foot with four toes that had sharp claws. It is believed to have fed on small mammals, reptiles, and other birds.

Ursus Spelarus

■ Lived about 30 million years ago ■

Ursus Spelarus, the cave-bear, was an ancestor of the modern-day bear. At almost 10 feet long, it was one of the largest mammals to live during its time period. It had very sharp teeth and long, sharp claws on its feet. It also had powerful legs that could easily move its bulky weight. It looked very fierce, but it did not feed on other animals. This cave-bear was a strict vegetarian.

Dinotherium

■ Lived about 13 million years ago ■

The Dinotherium was gigantic. It looked very much like an elephant, but was not a member of that family. It had no upper teeth, but its chin extended

down and held two downward-curving tusks. This animal probably ate by using its jaw. It probably swallowed every kind of vegetation with the help of its trunk. The Dinotherium lived mostly in Europe and Asia. But in Africa, it died out only about 500,000 years ago.

Megatherium

■ Lived about one million years ago ■

The Megatherium was a giant sloth that lived in North and South America. It became extinct about the time that the first European explorers came to the Americas. It was nearly as tall as an elephant and about 18 feet long. Its front paws had claws that could grab things. Its hind legs were massive. It had a powerful tail that it sometimes used as a fifth leg. This animal had no teeth and ate with the help of its tongue. It did not eat meat.

Mammoth

■ Lived about 50,000 years ago ■

The Mammoth is a prehistoric elephant. It is well known because a few were preserved by ice and found in Alaska and Siberia. The Mammoth lived in the Arctic areas. There, its thick fur protected it from the cold. It had huge tusks that bent backward and grew from the cheek bones beneath the eyes. These tusks sometimes grew to 13 feet long! Some Mammoths stood as high as 13½ feet, but most were smaller — only 6 feet tall.

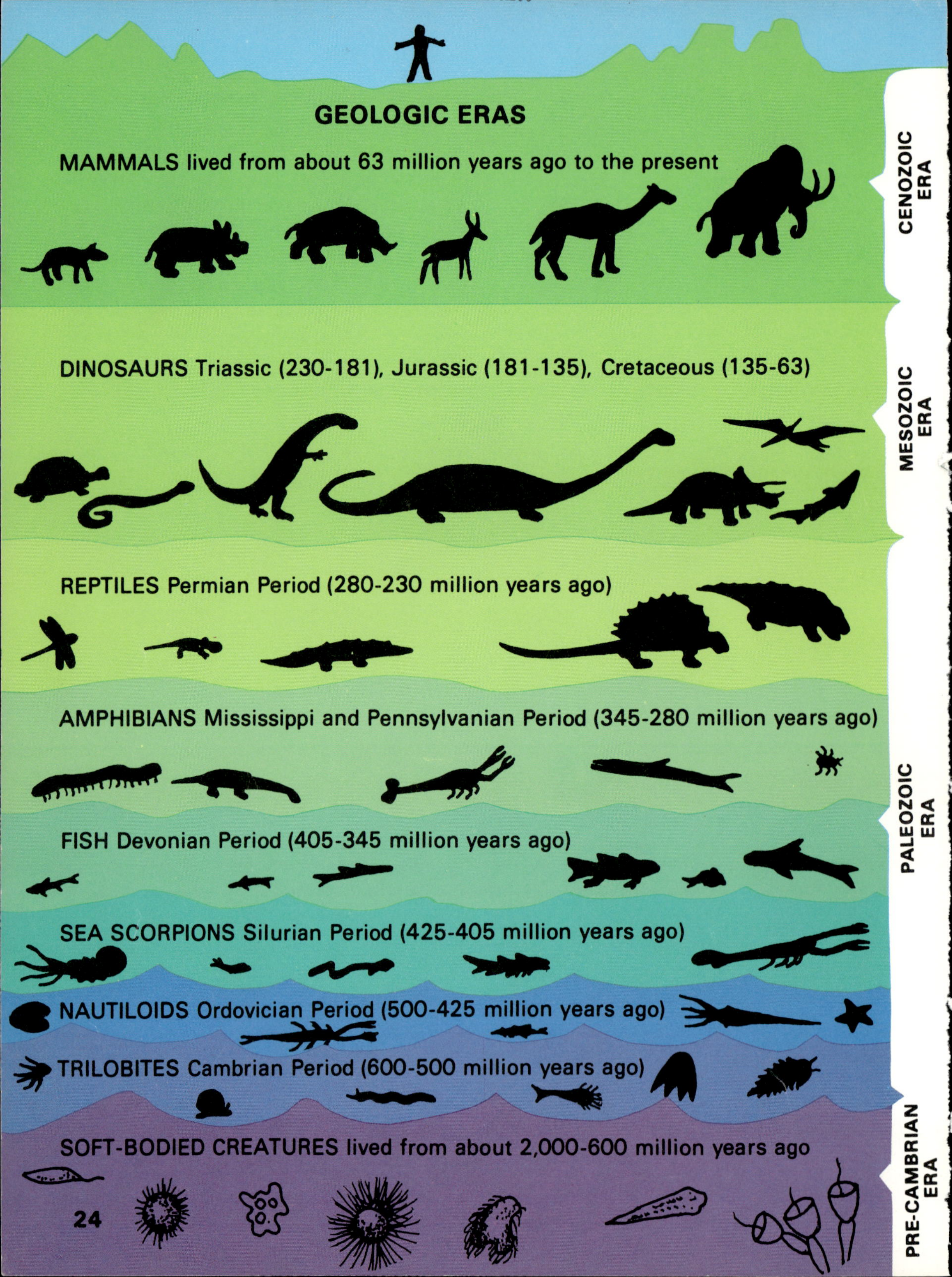
GEOLOGIC ERAS
MAMMALS lived from about 63 million years ago to the present
DINOSAURS Triassic (230-181), Jurassic (181-135), Cretaceous (135-63)
REPTILES Permian Period (280-230 million years ago)
AMPHIBIANS Mississippi and Pennsylvanian Period (345-280 million years ago)
FISH Devonian Period (405-345 million years ago)
SEA SCORPIONS Silurian Period (425-405 million years ago)
NAUTILOIDS Ordovician Period (500-425 million years ago)
TRILOBITES Cambrian Period (600-500 million years ago)
SOFT-BODIED CREATURES lived from about 2,000-600 million years ago
CENOZOIC ERA
MESOZOIC ERA
PALEOZOIC ERA
PRE-CAMBRIAN ERA

Contents

Farewell to Moab

"It is time for me to go back to my home in Bethlehem," Naomi said to Ruth and Orpah. Naomi's voice was kind as she talked, for she loved her daughters-in-law. Ruth and Orpah listened as Naomi continued. "You have been good to me while I lived in Moab. When you married Mahlon and Chilion, I was happy that my sons had chosen such fine young women as you two.

"But now we are all sad. Elimelech, my husband, has been dead for several years. And now Mahlon and Chilion are dead. Go back to the homes of your mothers. Perhaps there you will be able to find new husbands and raise families of your own."

Ruth looked at kind Naomi. She remembered long ago when the family had first come to Moab. In the midst of fighting and confusion, no crops had been harvested. There was no rain in Bethlehem and no food. Elimelech and Naomi and their two sons had come to Moab to find food.

The family had intended to stay for only a short time, but they had lived in Moab for ten years. Elimelech had died. Mahlon had married Ruth, and Chilion had married Orpah. Ruth loved Naomi very much. She knew that her mother-in-law was alone in the world now that her sons were dead.

"We will go to Bethlehem with you," said Ruth and Orpah.

"No, my daughters," Naomi said, "it will be best for you to stay here. Stay here where you will have a chance to marry again and raise families of your own. It is best that you remain here in Moab."

Orpah kissed Naomi. Then Orpah started back to her own home.

"Why are you still here, Ruth?" asked Naomi. "Orpah has gone home. You must go, too."

"Do not ask me to leave you, Naomi," Ruth said. "From now on I will go where you go, and my home will be where your home is. Your people will be my people. Your God will be my God."

Naomi was surprised. She knew that the people of Moab worshiped the idol Chemosh. Naomi was happy that Ruth had chosen to continue worshiping the true God.

Ruth went on. "I will stay with you until we both die."

Ruth knew that she had not chosen an easy task. It would be hard to leave her home, her family, her friends, and her customs. But Ruth loved Naomi. Ruth knew that God would give her the courage to begin a new life in Bethlehem.

Thinkback: Answer these questions:

Where was Naomi's home?

Where was Ruth's home?

Why had Naomi and her family come to Moab?

Whom did Naomi's people worship?

Whom did Ruth's people worship?

In what ways did Ruth show courage?

A New Home in Bethlehem

The late afternoon April sun warmed the tired bodies of Ruth and Naomi as they neared the village of Bethlehem.

"I am glad we are nearly home," spoke Naomi in a tired voice. "Our fifty-mile walk from Moab to Bethlehem has seemed very long."

"Yes," spoke Ruth quietly, "the journey

has been hard." Just ahead Ruth could see the quiet homes of Bethlehem. Surrounding the village were the barley fields that were ready for harvesting. On the west Ruth could see the rocky ridge, which was higher than the village. All around were orchards of fig trees and olive trees.

For a moment Ruth may have paused to look to the east. Ruth remembered her home. She could almost see the faces of her parents and friends.

Then Ruth looked at Naomi. "Let's hurry," said Ruth. "I am anxious to see your home in Bethlehem."

As the two women entered the village, they were met by the women of Bethlehem. "Can this be Naomi?" the women asked aloud. They remembered when Naomi, her husband, and their two sons had left Judah to go to Moab. The women could hardly believe that in these ten years Naomi had lost not only her husband but also her two sons.

"Perhaps God has punished Naomi for leaving Bethlehem and going to Moab where they worship the idol Chemosh," some of the women must have gossiped.

Naomi listened to the gossip of the women. Perhaps she felt sad and ashamed before her former neighbors. "My name used to be Naomi, which means pleasant," she said. "My new name is Mara, which means bitter. God has left Ruth and me

all alone."

Naomi knew that the life of a widow was very hard. She was sad that there would be no men in her family to plant the fields and harvest the grain. But Naomi was glad for the love shown to her by Ruth.

"Who is this woman Ruth that has come with you?" some of the women asked.

"Ruth is the widow of my son Mahlon," Naomi said. "She has come to live with me in Bethlehem. Ruth left her homeland, her family, and her friends. She now worships the true God. She has done these things to show her love for me."

"Ruth has shown great courage," the women said as Ruth and Naomi walked on.

That evening the two women ate a small meal in Naomi's house. "Bethlehem is far from Moab, Naomi," said Ruth, "but already I feel at home."

"I thank God that you are with me,"

said Naomi. "And now we must rest. Tomorrow we will think about getting food."

Thinkback: Answer these questions:

Why do you think Ruth decided to leave her home and go with Naomi?

How far did Ruth and Naomi travel from Moab to Bethlehem?

What time of year did Ruth and Naomi arrive in Bethlehem?

What did the women of the village think about Naomi?

Where did Ruth and Naomi stay in Bethlehem?

In what ways did Ruth show courage?

In the Fields of Boaz

Early the next morning Ruth woke and dressed quickly. "Naomi," Ruth said, "I will find food for us today. I will go to the fields where the workers are cutting grain. I will follow behind them and pick up the grain that they drop."

"Good," said Naomi. "It is our custom for widows and poor people to glean in the fields in that way. Go about your work. And God be with you."

Ruth hurried to the barley fields. The bright rays of the sun struck the tall, ripe grain. In the cool of the morning, reapers were already beginning to cut the stalks and gather the grain. Closely behind the reapers followed women who gathered grain left over by the quick, careless cuts of the reapers.

Ruth hurried to the place where the overseer of the reapers stood. "Please," she asked, "may I walk along behind the reapers and gather some of the fallen grain?"

When the overseer had given his permission, Ruth went quickly about her

work. She worked hard and was pleased as she saw her bundle of grain grow larger.

Later that day Boaz, the owner, came to the field. "God be with you," he said to the reapers.

"And God bless you," the men answered.

Boaz noticed Ruth picking up grain behind the reapers. "Who is that woman?" he asked his servant.

The servant explained that Ruth had arrived early in the morning asking

permission to gather grain. The servant explained, “She is the woman from Moab, the daughter-in-law of Naomi. She has worked very hard gathering grain.”

Quickly Boaz walked over to where Ruth was working. “Stay in my fields to do your gleaning of the grain,” he said. “I will tell the young men in my fields not to bother you in any way. And drink from the skin bottles of water when you are thirsty.”

Ruth kneeled at the feet of Boaz. “Oh, sir, why are you so kind to me, a stranger?’ she asked.

“I’ve heard good things about your kindness to Naomi, my relative,” said Boaz. “God will bless you because of your courage and trust in him.”

At mealtime, Boaz said to Ruth, "Come and eat parched grain with me and my workers."

All the rest of that day Ruth worked in the fields. Boaz had told his reapers to leave extra grain for Ruth. At the end of the day she had almost a bushel of grain

to carry home. She also had saved extra parched corn from her lunch.

Ruth hurried home to Naomi. "See all the grain," Ruth cried excitedly. Then she told Naomi about all that had happened that day.

"Why, Boaz is one of our nearest relatives," said Naomi. "Surely God has been with you this day. Do as Boaz says, and gather grain only in his fields."

That evening the two women ate the barley cakes made from the grain and shared the parched corn left from Ruth's lunch in the fields. Ruth and Naomi were full of hope and joy.

Thinkback: Answer these questions:

In whose fields did Ruth gather grain?

In what ways was Boaz kind to Ruth?

In what ways did Ruth show courage?

Courageous Ruth

All through the time of the barley harvest and the time of the wheat harvest Ruth worked. She gleaned grain in the fields of Boaz.

One evening as Ruth and Naomi shared their supper together, Naomi thought of a plan. "Tonight Boaz and his workers will be at the threshing floor."

Ruth had watched as the grain had been threshed that day on the hard, rocky floor in a space near the fields. She had seen the grain being separated from straw as the workers led oxen around the floor. Later the grain had been thrown high in the air. The chaff, or waste, had been blown away by the gentle winds. Piles of good grain lay on the threshing floor.

“Boaz and his men will be guarding the great piles of grain to keep any thieves from stealing the harvest,” said Naomi.

"After the men have finished their celebration meal, go to the place where Boaz will be sleeping. Be sure that no one sees you. When Boaz is sleeping soundly, lie down at his feet. Keep lying there until he wakens and tells you what to do."

"I will do what you have told me," said Ruth bravely. Ruth knew that what Naomi was asking her to do was strange, but Ruth trusted both Naomi and God. Later that night Ruth went quietly to the threshing floor where Boaz was asleep. Quietly she lay down at his feet.

About midnight, Boaz woke suddenly. He was very surprised to see a woman lying at his feet. "Who are you?" Boaz asked.

"I am Ruth," she answered.

Naomi had told Ruth of the law that said that a close relative should care for the widow of a kinsman who had died. Boaz also knew about this law.

"God bless you for coming to me, Ruth," Boaz answered. "You could have chosen another relative, but you have made me very happy by choosing me.

"Do not worry," Boaz continued, "for I will take care of you. I have heard everywhere in Bethlehem what a kind and courageous woman you are.

"Stay here tonight, and tomorrow I will talk to a relative that is closer to you than I am," said Boaz. "If he will not carry out the law and take care of you, I will have the honor of keeping the law. I will make

you my wife and will care for you and Naomi."

Ruth's heart sang with happiness. Early the next morning before others were awake, Ruth hurried home to Naomi. In her arms she carried a large load of barley sent by Boaz. Quickly she told Naomi all that had happened.

Naomi was very happy. "Wait patiently, Ruth," she advised. "Boaz will certainly take care of the matter this very day," Naomi promised.

Thinkback: Answer these questions:

What was Naomi's plan?
Where did Ruth find Boaz?
What promise did Boaz make to Ruth?
In what ways did Ruth show courage?

At the Village Gate

Early in the morning Boaz went to the village gate to wait. Soon the relative came on his way to the fields.

"Stop for a minute," Boaz called. "I have some business to discuss with you." Quickly Boaz called ten of the leaders of the village to be present as the business was carried out. Then the two men sat down together.

"Naomi, our relative who has just returned from Moab, has some land that she must sell," explained Boaz. "Do you, as the nearest relative, want to buy it?" asked Boaz. "If you do not want it, then I will buy it."

"Why, yes," said the man, "I would like to buy the land and add it to my fields."

"If you buy the land, you will also need to take on the responsibility of taking care of Ruth, the widow of Naomi's son," Boaz quickly explained.

"Oh, no," said the man. "I cannot do that because I have a family of my own to look after. You go ahead and buy the land for yourself."

In the custom of the day, the man took off his shoe and handed it to Boaz. In this way the ten men who witnessed the business deal would know that the man meant what he was saying.

With a happy smile, Boaz rose to talk to the ten leaders and other people who were outside the village gate.

"You have all seen and heard what has happened here today. Let it be known that I will buy the land of Naomi. And I will marry Ruth and take care of her."

"We are witnesses of what you have promised," said the leaders and the people. "God bless you and Ruth as you make your home together. May your home be filled with children. May your happiness together be famous throughout Bethlehem."

Thinkback: Answer these questions:

What business did Boaz discuss with the nearest relative of Naomi?

How did the man show that he was completing the business deal with Boaz?

What announcement did Boaz make to the leaders and to the people?

How did the people want God to bless Boaz and Ruth?

A Happy Home

Boaz and Ruth were married. All their neighbors were glad as they watched the happy couple about their work. And Naomi was especially glad because of the joy and love she saw in Ruth's eyes.

One day Ruth came to Naomi. "God has blessed me in a special way, Naomi," Ruth said excitedly. "Soon Boaz and I will be having a child. God has already blessed the child because you will be its grandmother."

Naomi helped Ruth as she made preparations for the baby. Then one day the cries of the baby filled the home. Boaz and Ruth thanked God for their healthy baby son.

The women of the village came to visit the happy family. After they had looked at the baby, the women talked to Naomi.

"God has been good to you, Naomi," they said. "He has blessed you in a special way by sending this grandson. And God has blessed you even more with your daughter-in-law, Ruth. Courageous Ruth has been better to you than seven sons. May God continue to be with you and your family."

Boaz and Ruth took good care of Obed, their son. Naomi also helped to care for the baby. The happy home was filled with love. The family members loved one another, but most of all they loved and honored God.

Obed, the son of Ruth and Boaz, grew to be a man. Later Obed had a son of his own. His name was Jesse, and he was the father of David. God later sent his own Son to earth as a member of the family of David. And in the list of ancestors of Jesus is included the name of Ruth, the courageous woman from Moab.

Thinkback: Answer these questions:

In what special way did God bless the home of Ruth and Boaz?

What was the name of the son of Ruth and Boaz?

The names of Ruth, Boaz, and Obed are listed in the Bible as ancestors for someone. Who is it?

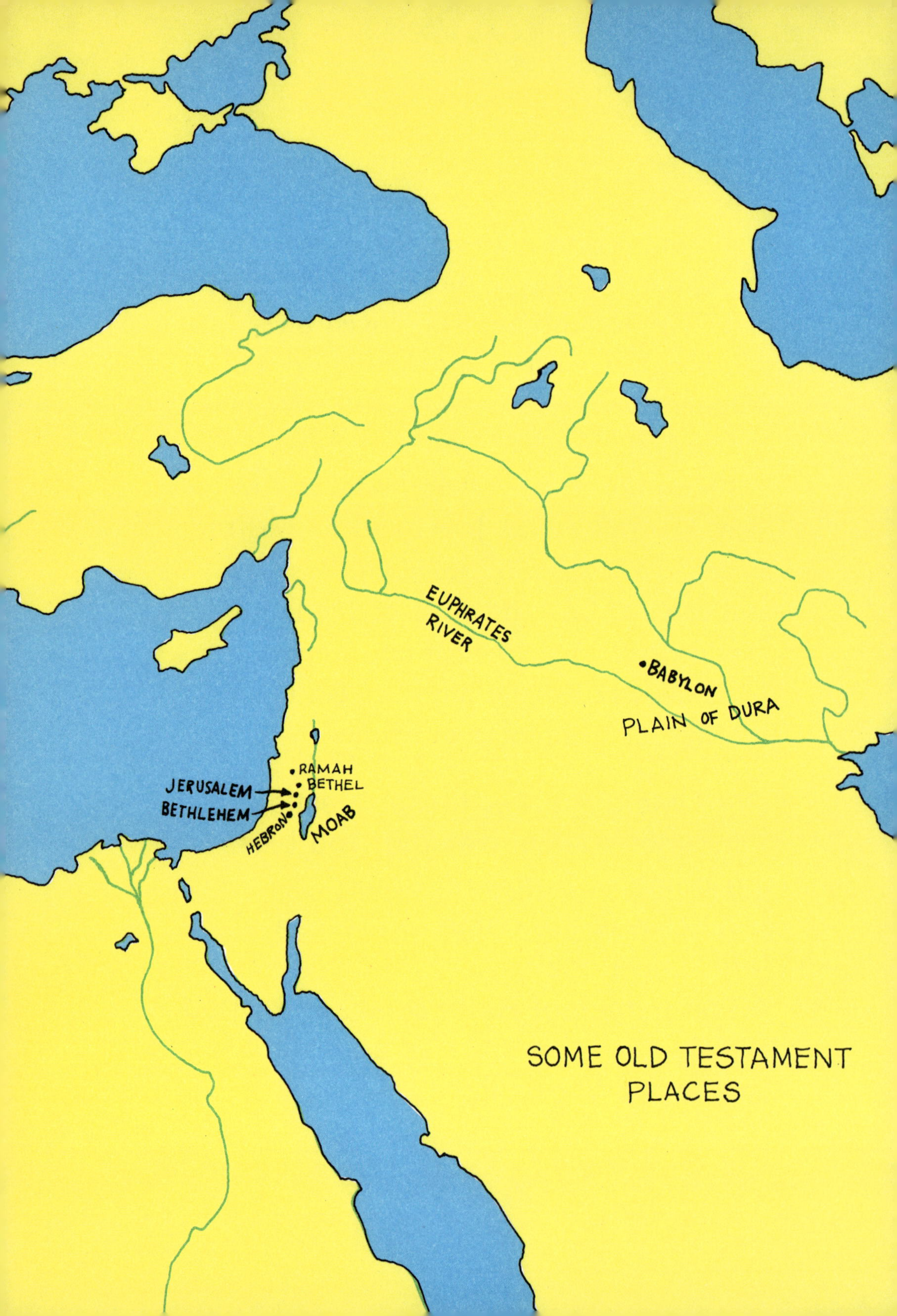

SOME OLD TESTAMENT PLACES

Reflections

Ruth, the stranger from Moab, became one of the ancestors of Jesus, God's own Son. Because of her courage, love, and devotion, Ruth is still remembered.

Ruth was courageous in many ways. She was ready to leave her home, her family, and her friends to move to a new land with Naomi. Unafraid, Ruth went to the fields to find food. Later Ruth followed Naomi's unusual instructions and went to the threshing floor at night.

Putting behind her the idol worship of her own people, Ruth trusted the one true God. And God honored Ruth's love and obedience by blessing her in a very special way.

You, too, can be courageous like Ruth. God can use you and bless you because of your obedience to him.

Think about your answers to these questions:

• How can you show your courage by making right choices even when it is hard?

• How can you treat others around you with love and respect?

• Are you one of God's followers? If you have not yet trusted Jesus as your Savior, ask God to help you know when it is time for you to follow him.

The story of Ruth is found in the book of Ruth in your Bible. Find and read all of Ruth's story in your own Bible. Pray that God will help you to be as courageous as Ruth.